Library
New Haven Elem

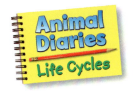

A Sea Turtle's Life

by
Ellen Lawrence

Consultant:

David Godfrey
Executive Director
Sea Turtle Conservancy
Gainesville, Florida

New York, New York

Credits

Cover, © idreamphoto/Shutterstock; 4, © mimagephotography/Shutterstock; 5, © David Evison/Shutterstock; 6, © David Evison/Shutterstock; 7, © OceanPhoto/FLPA; 8, © Ariadne Van Zandbergen/FLPA; 9, © incamerastock/Alamy; 10, © Kelvin Aitken/VWPICS/Alamy; 11, © Mark Conlin/Alamy; 12T, © Hiroya Minakuchi/Minden Pictures/FLPA; 12–13, © Tui De Roy/Minden Pictures/FLPA; 14–15, © Jordi Chias/Nature Picture Library; 16, © Rich Carey/Shutterstock; 17, © David Fleetham/Alamy; 19, © M. Swiet Productions/Pacific Stock/Alamy; 20, © Tammy Wolfe/Alamy; 21, © Colin Marshall/FLPA; 23TL, © PRILL/Shutterstock; 23TC, © tropicdreams/Shutterstock; 23TR, © Erika Antoniazzo/Alamy; 23BL, © Ocean Image Photography/Shutterstock; 23BC, © Hiroya Minakuchi/Minden Pictures/FLPA; 23BR, © Matt Jeppson/Shutterstock.

Publisher: Kenn Goin
Editor: Jessica Rudolph
Creative Director: Spencer Brinker
Design: Emma Randall
Photo Researcher: Ruby Tuesday Books Ltd

Library of Congress Cataloging-in-Publication Data

Names: Lawrence, Ellen, 1967– author. | Lawrence, Ellen, 1967– Animal diaries.
Title: A sea turtle's life / by Ellen Lawrence.
Description: New York, New York : Bearport Publishing, [2017] | Series: Animal diaries: life cycles | Audience: Ages 6-10. | Includes bibliographical references and index.
Identifiers: LCCN 2016012088 (print) | LCCN 2016018526 (ebook) | ISBN 9781944102487 (library binding) | ISBN 9781944997410 (ebook)
Subjects: LCSH: Green turtle—Life cycles—Juvenile literature. | Green turtle—Behavior—Juvenile literature. | Sea turtles—Juvenile literature.
Classification: LCC QL666.C536 L39 2017 (print) | LCC QL666.C536 (ebook) | DDC 597.92/8—dc23
LC record available at https://lccn.loc.gov/2016012088

Copyright © 2017 Bearport Publishing Company, Inc. All rights reserved. No part of this publication may be reproduced in whole or in part, stored in any retrieval system, or transmitted in any form or by any means, electronic, mechanical, photocopying, recording, or otherwise, without written permission from the publisher.

For more information, write to Bearport Publishing Company, Inc., 45 West 21st Street, Suite 3B, New York, New York 10010. Printed in the United States of America.

Contents

Meet a Green Sea Turtle............4
Turtle Eggs......................6
Keeping the Eggs Safe 8
The Turtle Babies Hatch...........10
Run, Babies, Run!................. 12
A Hatchling's Life 14
Adult Turtles......................... 16
Swimming Around................... 18
A Special Journey.................... 20

Science Lab 22
Science Words 23
Index 24
Read More 24
Learn More Online 24
About the Author 24

Name: **Dylan**   Date: **June 1**

Meet a Green Sea Turtle

Today, I saw a green sea turtle near my home in Florida.

I was on the beach with my older brother, who's a turtle scientist.

The **reptile** had crawled out of the sea and onto the beach.

Then it began to dig a hole in the sand.

Dylan

■ Where green sea turtles live

A green sea turtle can weigh up to 400 pounds (181 kg). Its bony shell can be 4 feet (1.2 m) long.

green sea turtle

How do you think green sea turtles dig holes?

Date: June 2

Turtle Eggs

My brother said the turtle was a female making a nest.

She used her flippers to dig a large hole in the sand.

Next, she began laying eggs in the hole.

She laid 115 eggs in total!

Then she used her flippers to cover the eggs with sand.

flipper

a sea turtle digging a nest

nest hole

eggs

A sea turtle egg is about the size of a ping-pong ball. It has a soft, leathery shell.

What do you think a female turtle does after she's laid her eggs?

Date: June 3

Keeping the Eggs Safe

After laying her eggs, the sea turtle crawled back into the ocean.

Beneath the sand, the baby turtles are starting to grow inside their eggs.

My brother put special tape around the turtle nest.

This keeps people from disturbing the nest below the sand.

It's important that the eggs are kept safe because green sea turtles are **threatened**.

a female turtle crawling back to the sea

The turtle nest is under the sand.

Turtles are threatened for many reasons. Sometimes they become tangled in fishing nets and then drown.

Date: **August 2**

The Turtle Babies Hatch

It's been two months since the mother turtle laid her eggs.

Today, my brother listened for scratching noises under the sand.

He said the babies were hatching from their eggs!

Suddenly, several tiny, black turtle heads popped out of the sand.

The little **hatchlings** had dug their way to the surface.

a baby turtle digging to the surface

A newly hatched turtle's shell is about 2 inches (5 cm) long. The hatchling weighs about 0.9 ounce (26 g). That's about the same weight as five quarters.

What do you think the babies will do once they have left their underground nest?

Date: **August 2**

Run, Babies, Run!

Once the hatchlings were out of their nest, they were off!

Each one crawled as fast as it could toward the ocean.

It's a dangerous time for the babies.

Seabirds and other **predators** try to catch and eat the tiny hatchlings.

When the babies reach the water, they swim away from the shore.

a heron eating a hatchling

Turtle hatchlings have no parent to lead them to the ocean. They somehow know which way to crawl as soon as they hatch.

In what ways does a hatchling look similar to its mother? In what ways is it different?

Date: September 3

A Hatchling's Life

It's been a month since the baby turtles left the beach.

My brother explains that they are living out at sea.

The baby turtles hunt for small crabs, shrimp, and insects near the surface of the water.

Not all the turtles will survive, though.

Many will be eaten by seabirds, sharks, and other large fish.

A sea turtle comes to the surface about once every five minutes to breathe. However, when it sleeps under water, it can go for four hours without taking a breath of air!

a young green sea turtle

Date: May 1

Adult Turtles

Today, my brother and I went swimming in the ocean and saw a large turtle feeding on plants.

Could it be one of the babies all grown up?

My brother said no, because sea turtles grow very slowly.

It can take 25 years before they are fully grown!

Adult sea turtles only eat sea grass and plant-like **algae**.

sea grass

A green sea turtle has no teeth. Instead, it has hard, saw-like ridges that help it munch on plants.

a diver taking a picture of a sea turtle

How do you think green sea turtles got their name?

17

Date: May 2

Swimming Around

My brother has taught me all about the lives of green sea turtles.

He said a turtle moves from one area of the sea to another to search for food.

It might swim hundreds of miles in just one year!

Adult turtles usually live on their own in the ocean.

However, sometimes female and male turtles meet up to **mate**.

Green sea turtles got their name because the flesh under their shells is green. The green sea grass and algae they eat turns their flesh green.

After mating, a female green sea turtle will go back to the beach where she hatched. Why do you think she does this?

Date: July 31

A Special Journey

It's been nearly a year since I saw the little hatchlings swim out to sea.

One day, in about 24 years, some of them will return to this beach. Why?

Female turtles come back to the beach where they hatched so they can lay their own eggs.

I'll be a grown-up when I see those turtles again!

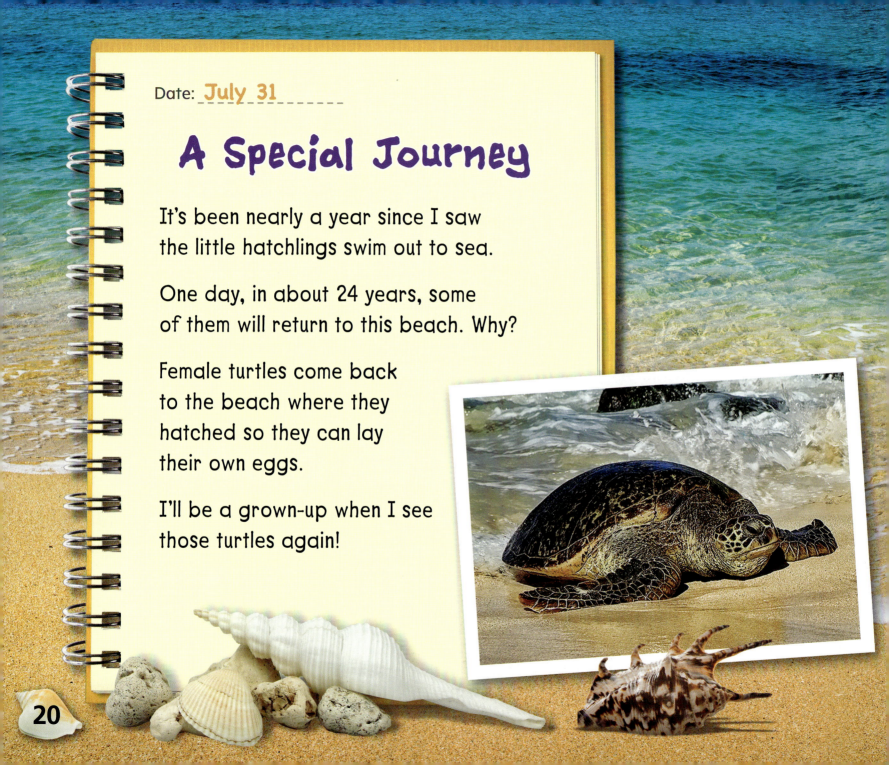

An adult female turtle lays eggs every two years.

a scientist measuring an adult female green sea turtle

How long do you think a green sea turtle can live for?
(The answer is on page 24.)

Science Lab

Help Save Sea Turtles

Make a poster that tells people about the dangers that sea turtles face. Some reasons they are threatened include:

- People catch and eat sea turtles. They also eat turtle eggs.

- People build hotels, shops, and homes on beaches. Then sea turtles cannot lay their eggs on these beaches.

- Sea turtles drown when they become trapped in fishing nets.

- People dump chemicals in the sea. This damages the turtles' ocean home.

- Sea turtles can be harmed or killed when they get tangled in plastic bags and other trash that people throw into the ocean.

On your poster, draw a green sea turtle.

Then write facts and draw pictures that explain one or more ways in which turtles can be harmed.

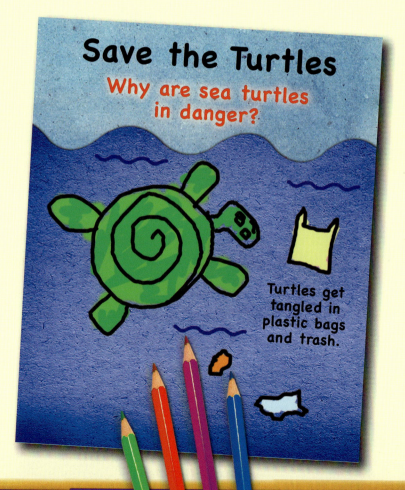

Science Words

algae (AL-jee) plant-like living things, such as seaweed, that are often found in ponds, lakes, rivers, and oceans

hatchlings (HACH-lingz) baby animals that have just hatched from their eggs

mate (MAYT) to come together to produce young

predators (PRED-uh-turz) animals that hunt other animals for food

reptile (REP-tile) a cold-blooded animal, such as a lizard, snake, or turtle, that has scaly skin

threatened (THRET-uhnd) having an uncertain chance of surviving

Index

dangers 8–9, 12, 14, 22
eggs 6–7, 8, 10, 20–21, 22
flippers 6
Florida 4

food 14, 16, 18
hatchlings 10–11, 12–13, 14, 20
mating 18–19

nests 6–7, 8–9, 11, 12
predators 12, 14
shells 5, 11

Read More

Blomquist, Christopher. *Green Sea Turtles (The Library of Turtles and Tortoises).* New York: Rosen (2004).

Owen, Ruth. *Sea Turtle Hatchlings (Water Babies).* New York: Bearport (2013).

Spilsbury, Louise. *Sea Turtle (A Day in the Life: Sea Animals).* Chicago: Heinemann Library (2011).

Learn More Online

To learn more about green sea turtles, visit www.bearportpublishing.com/AnimalDiaries

About the Author

Ellen Lawrence lives in the United Kingdom. Her favorite books to write are those about animals. In fact, the first book Ellen bought for herself when she was six years old was the story of a gorilla named Patty Cake that was born in New York's Central Park Zoo.

Answer for page 21

Scientists think green sea turtles can live to be 100 years old!